THE WORLD'S BEST DAD

Frances Lincoln
Children's Books

ME AND MY DAD

My dad's name is ....

He is .... years old and he

was born on .... My dad is

from .... and lives in

....

He likes ....

and ....

My favorite thing about my dad is ....

.... I'm giving him

this book because ....

A DRAWING OF DAD AND ME

DAD FACT #1
Some frog fathers keep their tadpoles in their mouths until they're ready to swim out on their own!

WHO WE ARE

Dad, below I've used one color to draw lines between words
that describe you, and another color to match words that describe me.
We're all of them and more!

DAD'S COLOR: ⬤   **MY COLOR:** ⬤

Caring	Friend
Funny	Neighbor
Loving	Teacher
Calm	Athlete
Smart	Musician
Cool	Artist
Talented	Scientist
Strong	Adventurer
Creative	Storyteller
Patient	Listener
Kind	Mathematician

Some ways you and I
are totally the same:

Some ways you and I
are totally different:

And we're both *PERFECT*
the way we are!

OLD MEMORIES

A special memory I have with you is ...

....

....

....

....

....

....

....

Here is
a drawing of that
SPECIAL DAY

DAD FACT #2
A father
emperor penguin
withstands the
Antarctic cold
for 60 days or
more to protect
his eggs!

NEW MEMORIES

Something I'd like to do with you one day is ...

....

....

....

....

....

....

....

Here is
a drawing of that
SPECIAL DAY

ANIMAL DADS QUIZ

The animal kingdom is full of amazing dads who
care for their young in a lot of different ways.
Take this quiz, then find out which animal dad
yours is most like on the next page!

Read each question, then pick an answer by circling A, B, or C.

1. You want to plan a day out with your dad for a special occasion. Would he prefer ...

A. A long, sweaty hike to a spectacular hilltop.
B. A class where you learn to cook exciting new foods.
C. A visit to an exhibition by his favorite artist (other than you, of course!).

2. You finish second in a race at school, and your dad is there to pick you up. Does he ...

A. Challenge you to a race himself, to see who's fastest!
B. Tell you he's proud of you and that second place is a great result.
C. Listen carefully as you talk through your frustration at not winning.

3. Your dad tells a story about a knight who defeats a dragon. How does the knight win?

A. She uses a magic sword to slay the dragon.
B. She outsmarts the dragon in a contest of riddles.
C. She talks to the dragon and they become best friends.

4. You and your dad are at home on a Sunday afternoon. What do you get up to?

A. An unplanned trip to the beach.
B. Helping each other out on a DIY project.
C. Spotting wildlife in the yard.

5. Your dad is helping you on a science project. What does he suggest you do?

A. Make a volcano using baking soda and vinegar. The messier, the better.
B. Analyze the cells of a plant. Any excuse to use a microscope!
C. Collect worms in a jar and build a wormery, then release them.

IF YOU ANSWERED MOSTLY A, YOUR DAD IS: **A SAND GROUSE!**

These birds travel hundreds of miles to find water for their chicks. Playful and outgoing, your dad likes nothing more than a big adventure.

IF YOU ANSWERED MOSTLY B, YOUR DAD IS: **A GORILLA!**

These great apes are leaders and teachers to their young. Your dad is always ready with the perfect piece of wisdom to share.

IF YOU ANSWERED MOSTLY C, YOUR DAD IS: **AN AROWANA!**

These fish keep their young safe—in their mouths! Your dad is caring, kind, and there for you when you need him.

IF YOU ANSWERED A AS MUCH AS B, YOUR DAD IS: A WOLF!

Wolf dads teach their cubs to find food. Your dad knows that every adventure has a lesson, and every lesson is an adventure!

IF YOU ANSWERED B AS MUCH AS C, YOUR DAD IS: A MARMOSET!

These monkey dads carry their young everywhere they go. Sensitive and wise, your dad sets an example for you to follow.

IF YOU ANSWERED C AS MUCH AS A, YOUR DAD IS: AN ELEPHANT!

Elephants form lifelong friendships with their young in roaming groups. Your dad believes the most exciting times make for the strongest bonds.

My dad is _____

ONCE UPON A TIME WITH DAD

Pick some words that fit the descriptions below, then add them to the story on the opposite page.

1. Somewhere familiar: ....

2. Something that flies: ....

3. A scary monster: ....

4. Something huge: ....

5. Someone my dad and I love: ....

6. A magical object: ....

7. A delicious food: ....

DAD FACT #3
The male South American rhea, a type of large flightless bird, looks after around fifty chicks all by himself!

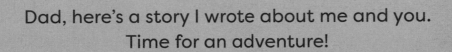

Dad, here's a story I wrote about me and you.
Time for an adventure!

"Once upon a time, my dad and I were walking in

_____ [1]. Suddenly, a monstrous

_____ [3] appeared! It was as big as

_____ [4]. It scooped us up and took

us to its lair on a magic _____ [2].

The _____ [3] kept saying it would

eat us, but my dad wasn't scared. He simply

phoned _____ [5] for help. Together,

they used a special _____ [6]

to scare the _____ [3] away. We

all rode the _____ [2] back to

_____ [1], where we sat down to a

well-deserved feast of _____ [7]—

our favorite! The End."

MY DAD'S DREAM MENU

Dad, here are the foods I'd put on the menu of your dreams. I've drawn pictures to show how delicious everything looks!

BREAKFAST

LUNCH

DINNER

APPETIZER

....

....

ENTRÉE

....

....

DESSERT

....

....

DAD FACT #4
Red fox fathers hide food close to their dens to
teach their pups how to forage and hunt.

A MAP OF ME AND DAD

Draw, write, and collage on these pages to create a cloud of everything that makes you and your dad special.

Draw or glue a picture of
you and your dad here.

WORLD'S BEST DAD

Dad, here are just some of the things you're great at:

☐ Meeting people

☐ Making people laugh

☐ Writing

☐ Building

☐ Fixing things

☐ Solving problems

☐ Jogging

☐ Gardening

☐ Swimming

☐ Cooking

☐ Drawing

☐ Climbing

☐ Relaxing

☐ Napping

☐ Sports

☐ Inventing

☐ Biking

☐ Exploring

☐ Singing

DAD FACT #5
Seahorse dads get pregnant and give birth.

But you're the *WORLD'S BEST* at

_____

Here's a *WORLD'S BEST DAD* mug I designed, just for you!

If we won a trophy together for being the best at something, here's what it would look like.

THEN AND NOW

Dad, you've been so many things in
your life—you inspire me every day!
When you were my age, you were:

1. ....
   ....
   ....
   ....

2. ....
   ....
   ....
   ....

3. ....
   ....
   ....
   ....

4. ....
   ....
   ....
   ....

When I'm your age, I want to be:

1. ....

2. ....

3. ....

4. ....

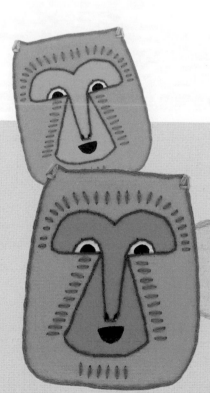

DAD FACT #6
Barbary macaques show off to others by parading
their little monkeys around on their backs.
Now, that's a proud dad!

DAD, YOU'RE MY HERO!
(AND EVERYONE KNOWS YOU'RE SUPER)

BUT IF YOU WERE A REAL SUPERHERO, YOUR POWER WOULD BE ...

○ Flight   ○ Laser vision   ○ Super strength

○ Mind-reading   ○ Being a genius   ○ Talking to animals

or _____

YOUR SUPERHERO HEADQUARTERS WOULD BE ...

○ A medieval castle   ○ A high-tech mansion   ○ A breezy treehouse

○ A cozy cabin   ○ An alien spaceship   ○ A backyard shed

or _____

YOUR SIDEKICK WOULD BE ...

○ A giant robot   ○ A dog that can fly   ○ An invisible friend

○ A 1,000-year-old wizard   ○ The world's fastest turtle   ○ Me!

or _____

SUPERDAD

YOUR SUPERHERO NAME IS

_____

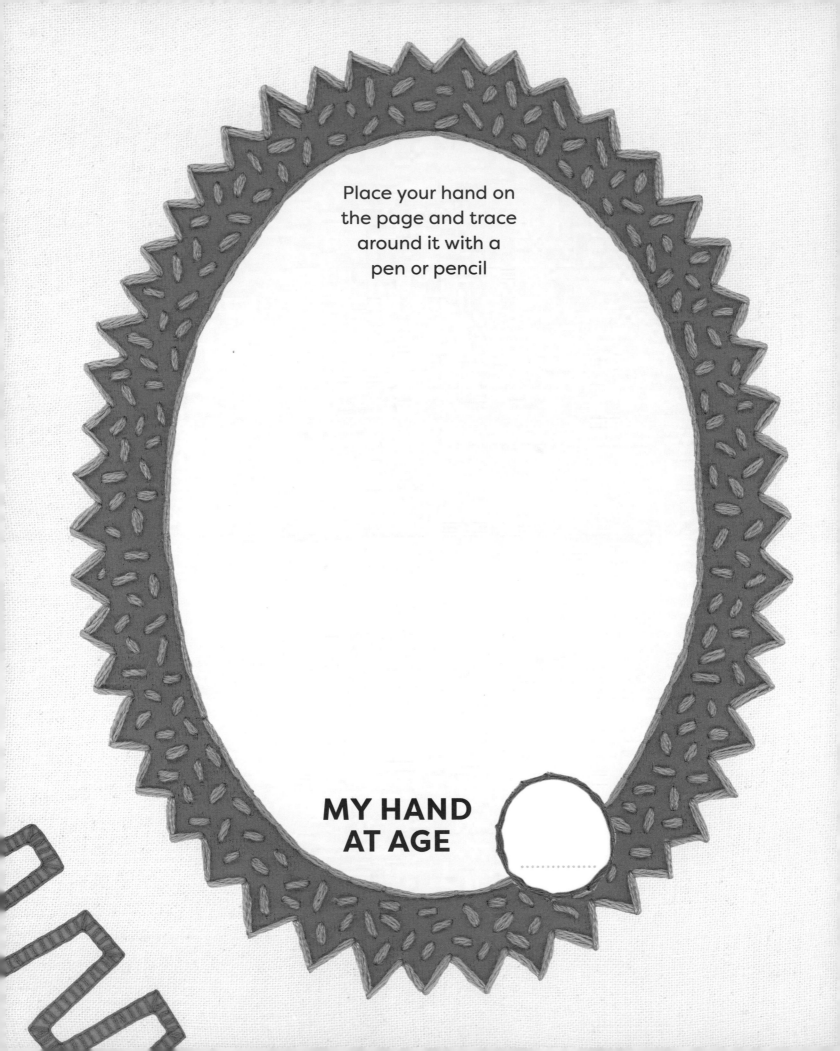

Place your hand on the page and trace around it with a pen or pencil

MY HAND AT AGE

When you give this book to your dad,
ask him to do the same on this page

**DAD'S HAND
AT AGE**

THE THINGS I LOVE MOST ABOUT YOU

1. ....
   ....

2. ....
   ....

3. ....
   ....

4. ....
   ....

5. ....
   ....

THREE LESSONS YOU HAVE TAUGHT ME

1. ....

....

....

2. ....

....

....

....

....

3. ....

....

....

....

....

....

PHOTO JOURNAL

Dad, here are some special pictures so we can always remember the memories we've shared so far. Here's to many more!

DAD FACT #8
The better a nightingale dad is at singing, the more protective he'll be of his chicks.

The
Quarto
Group

Inspiring | Educating | Creating | Entertaining

Brimming with creative inspiration, how-to
projects, and useful information to enrich your
everyday life, quarto.com is a favorite destination
for those pursuing their interests and passions.

First published in 2023 by Frances Lincoln Children's Books, an imprint of The Quarto Group.
100 Cummings Center, Suite 265D, Beverly, MA 01915, USA.
T +1 978-282-9590 **www.quarto.com**

A CIP record for this book is available from the Library of Congress.

ISBN 978-0-7112-7584-3

The illustrations were embroidered with thread, needle, and acrylic
Set in Wisely, Simone, Filson Pro

Published by Peter Marley
Designed by Kat Davies and Karissa Santos
Edited by Alex Hithersay
Production by Chris Tucker

Manufactured in Guangzhou, China. EB122022

9 8 7 6 5 4 3 2 1

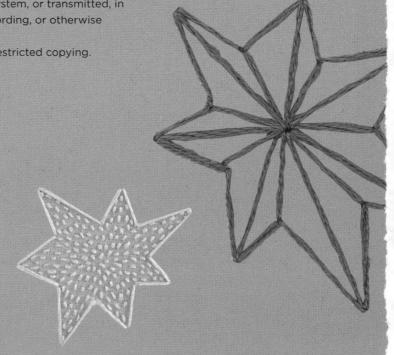